D0769356

How to Be Alone

How to Be Alone

Poem by Tanya Davis
With Illustrations by Andrea Dorfman

HARPER

www.harpercollins.com

For You

HarperCollins books may be purchased for educational, business, or sales promotional use. For information, please e-mail the Special Markets Department at SPsales@harpercollins.com.

First Edition

Designed by Andrea Dorfman

Library of Congress Cataloging-in-Publication Data has been applied for.

ISBN: 978-0-06-228084-8

13 14 15 16 17 AV/RRD 10 9 8 7 6 5 4 3 2 1

Our thanks to
BravoFACT for supporting the initial pro-
duction of the video poem "How to Be Alone";
Denise Bukowski for supporting its move
to the page; Maya Ziv, our wonderful editor
at HarperCollins; Claire Cameron for her
guidance; and our friends and families
for their support. "How to Be Alone" first
appeared in print in "At First, Lonely." a
collection of poems by Tanya Davis. pub-
lished by Acorn Press in 2011 (and thanks
to Jerilee Bulge for that).

If you
are at
first
lonely,

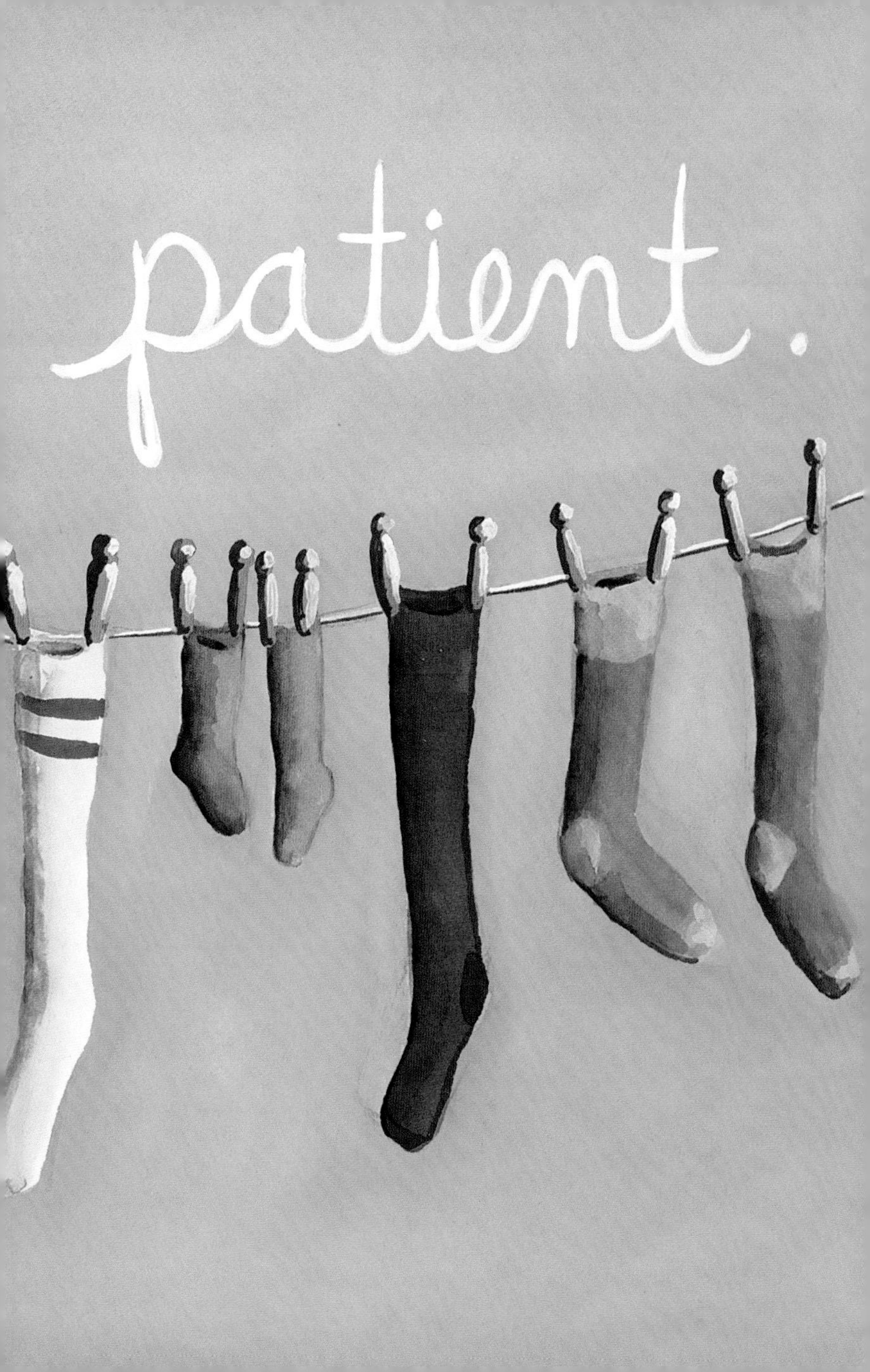
patient.

or if
when you were,
you weren't okay
with it,

once
you're
embracing
it.

We could start
with the
acceptable
places:

the

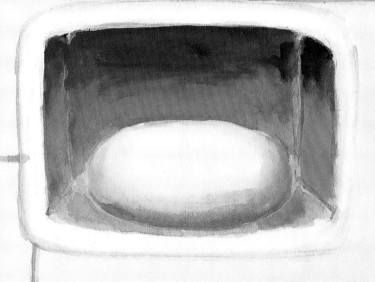

bathroom

where you can
stall and read
the paper,

where you can
get the caffeine
fix and sit
and stay
there,

where you can browse the stacks and smell the books.

you're not supposed to talk much anyway, so it's safe there.

If you're shy,
You can hang out
with yourself in mirrors;

And there's
public transportation
because we all
gotta go places.

And there's prayer and meditation;

no one will
think less
if you're
hanging
with your
breath
seeking
peace and
salvation.

Start

simple.

Things you may have previously avoided

based on your
avoid - being - alone
principles.

The lunch counter,

where you will
be surrounded by
chow-downers,

and their spouses work across town,

and so they,

will be

like you,

alone.

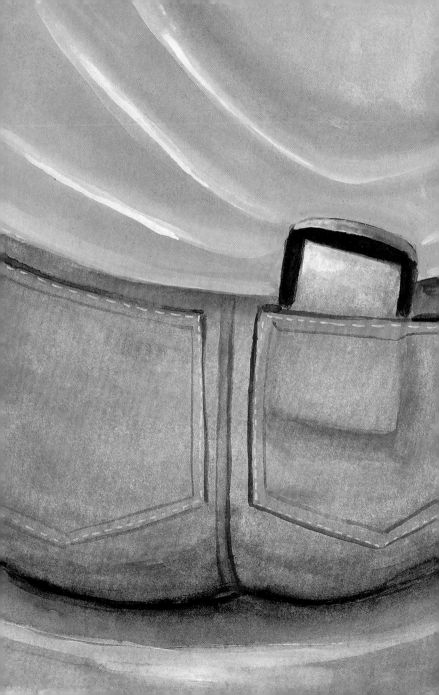

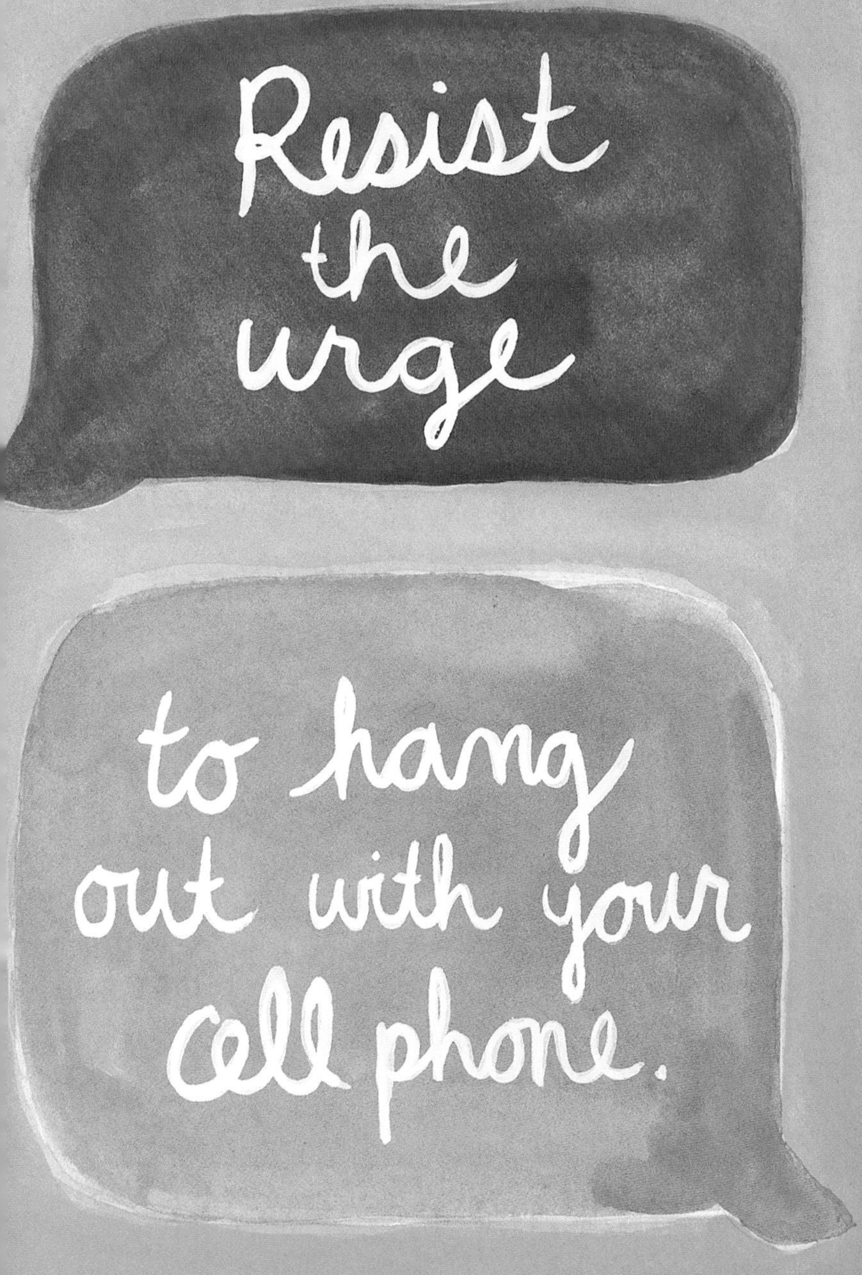
Resist the urge
to hang out with your cell phone.

When comfortable with
take yourself out

eat lunch and run,

for dinner

to a restaurant with linen and silverware.

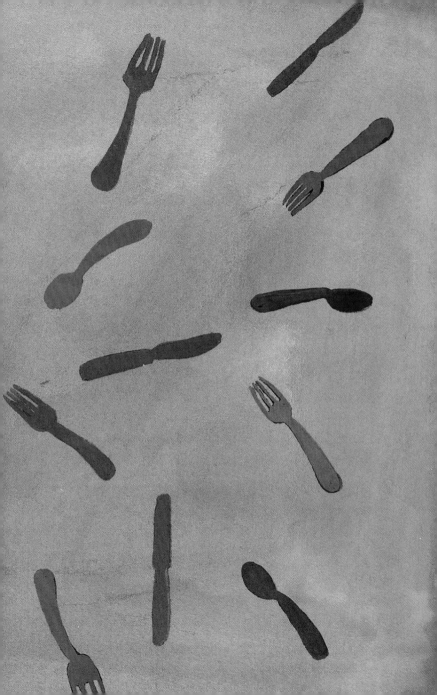

You're
no less
intriguing
a person

when you're eating
solo dessert
and cleaning the
whipped cream
from the dish
with your
finger;

will wish
they were
where you were.

Go to the movies

where it is
dark
and
soothing,

alone in
amid
fleeting

And then
take yourself
out dancing

to a club
where no one
knows you.

Stand on the floor until convince you

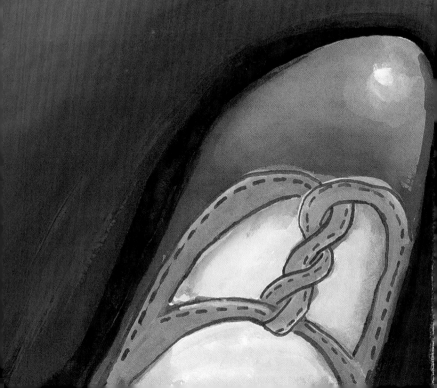

outside of the
the lights

more and more

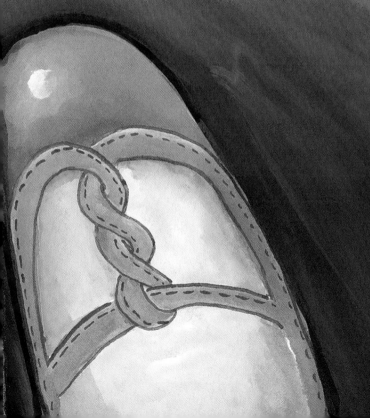

and the music

shows you.

Dance like no one's watching

because they're probably not.

And if they are,
with the best

The way bodies
beats is, after all,

assume it is
of human intentions.
move genuinely to
gorgeous and affecting.

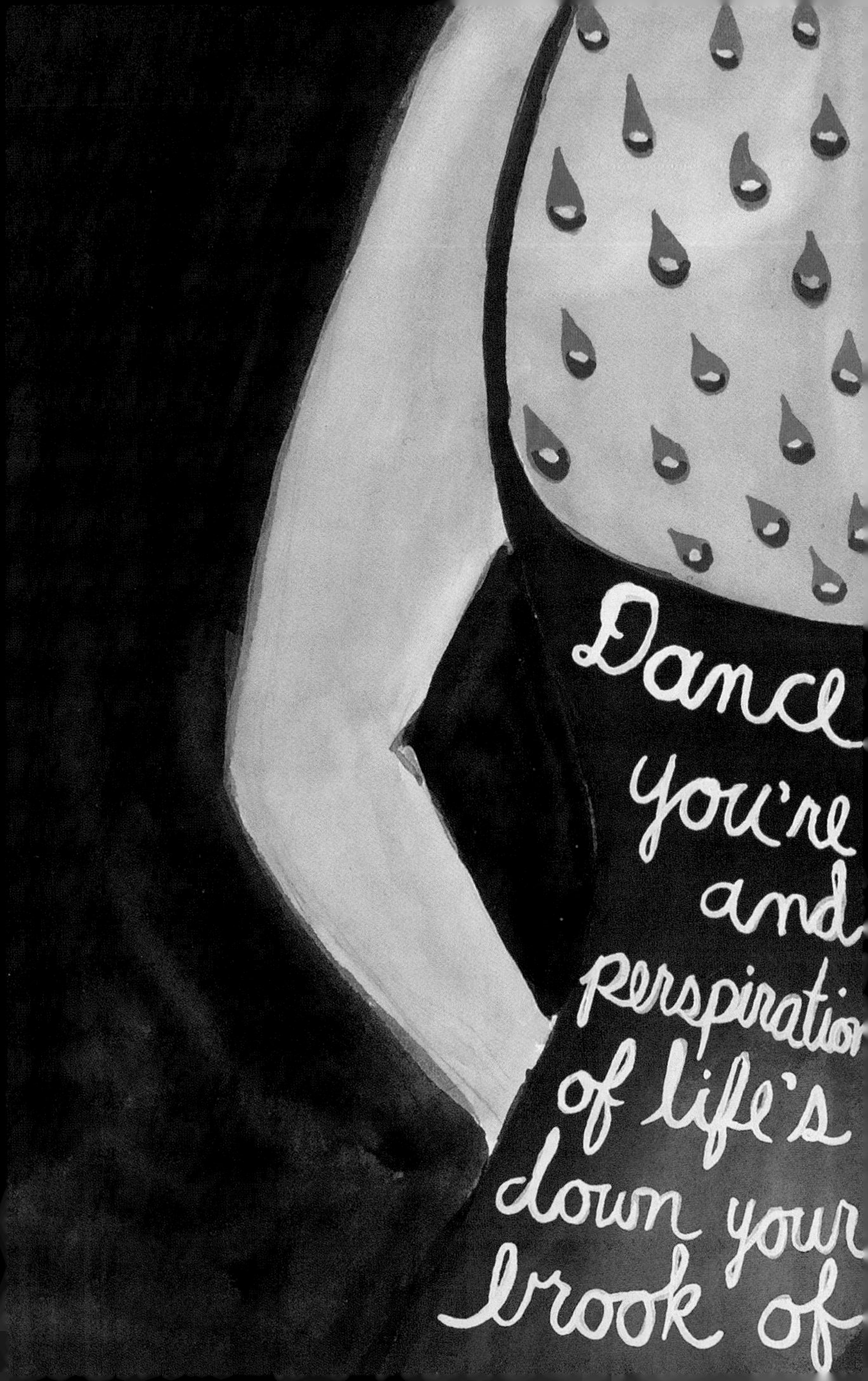
Dance
you're
and
perspiratio
of life's
down your
brook of

until
sweating
beads of
remind you
best things
back like a
blessings.

Go to the woods alone,

where trees
and squirrels
will watch for you.

Go to
an unfamiliar

city; roam the streets.

And benches made

give strangers a

if only for
and these moments

might have.
never happened
had you not
been there
by yourself.

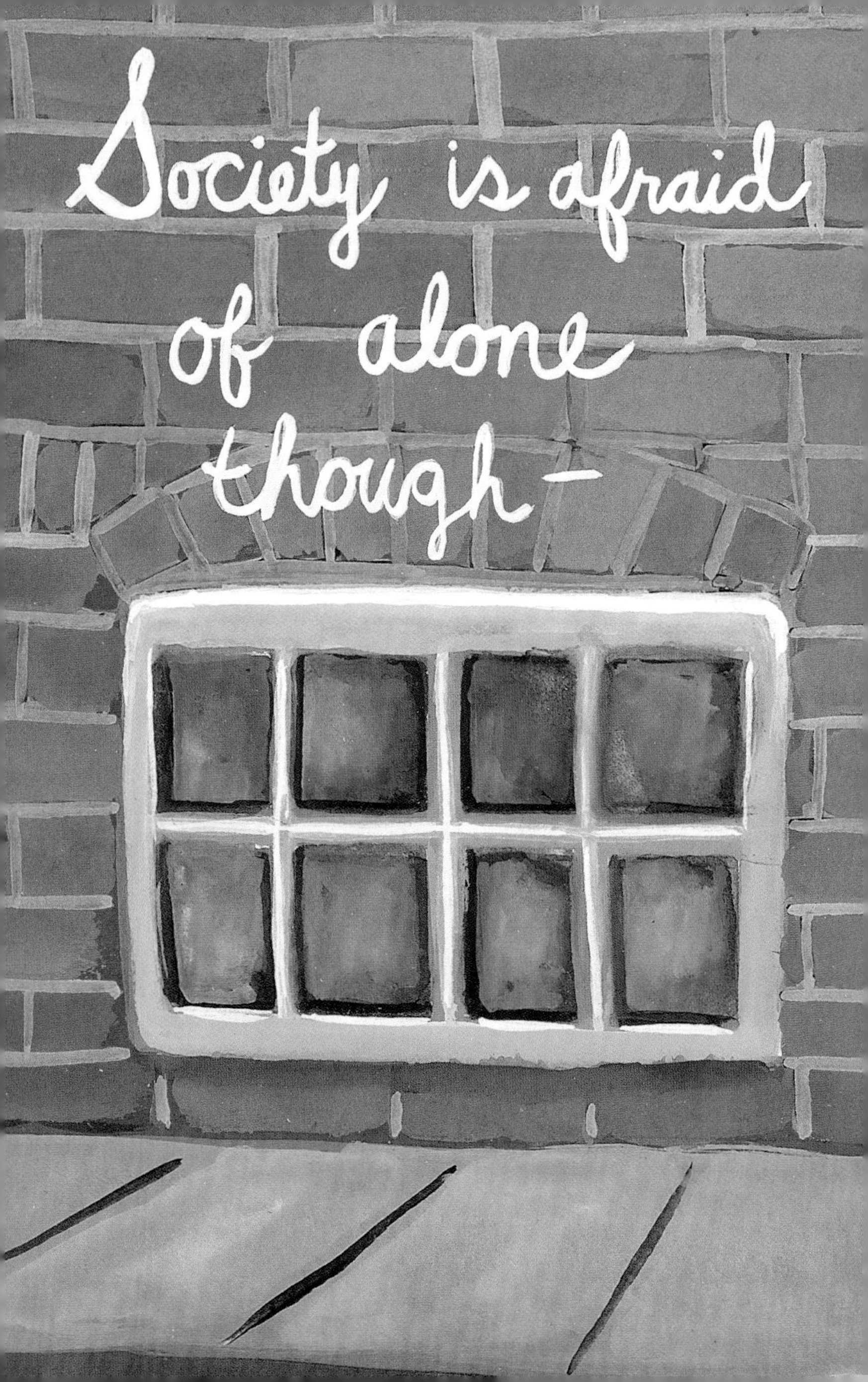
Society is afraid
of alone
though –

like lonely hearts
are wasting away
in basements,

like people
must have problems
if after a while
no one's dating them.

But alone is a
freedom that breathes
easy and
weightless,

and lonely
is healing if you
make it.

you could stand swathed by groups and mobs,

look both
further and
farther

in the
endless quest
for
company.

But no one's
and by the
translate

in your head,
time you
your thoughts,

some essence
of them
may be lost,

or perhaps
it is just
kept,

perhaps
in the interest
of loving
oneself.

Perhaps all of
those sappy slogans
from preschool
over to high school's
groaning
were tokens for
holding

the
lonely
at
bay.

'Cause if you're happy in your head, then solitude is blessed

and alone is okay.

It's okay if

believes

all experiences

no one

like you,

are unique,

no one has
the same
synapses,

can't think
like you,
for this be
relieved,

And it

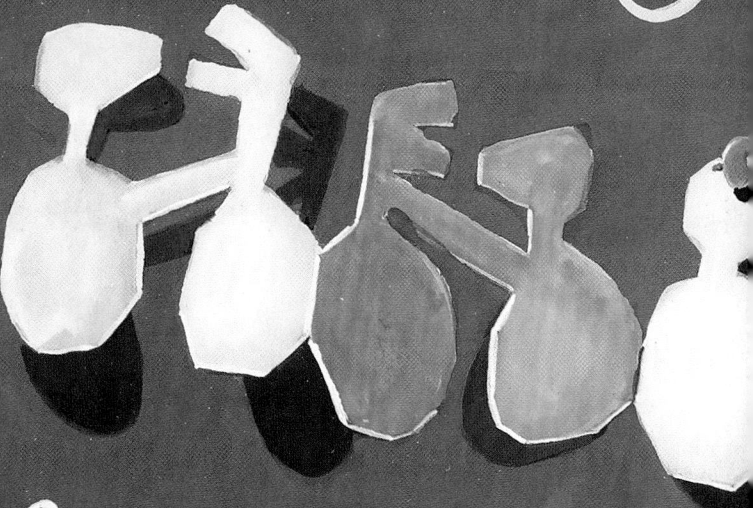

mean you
connected,
community's

doesn't

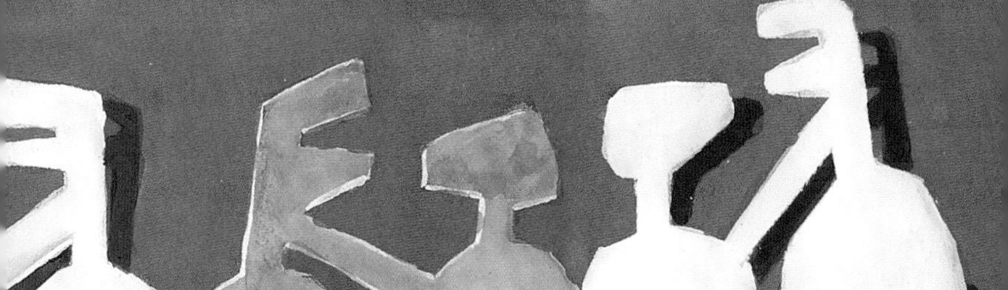

aren't
that
not present.

Just take the
perspective
you get from

being one person
alone
in one head
and feel the
effects of it.

Take silence

and respect it.

If you have an art that needs a practice,

If your family doesn't get you or a religious sect is not meant for you. obsess it.

You could,
in an instant,
be surrounded

If your
heart
is
bleeding,

make
the best
of it.

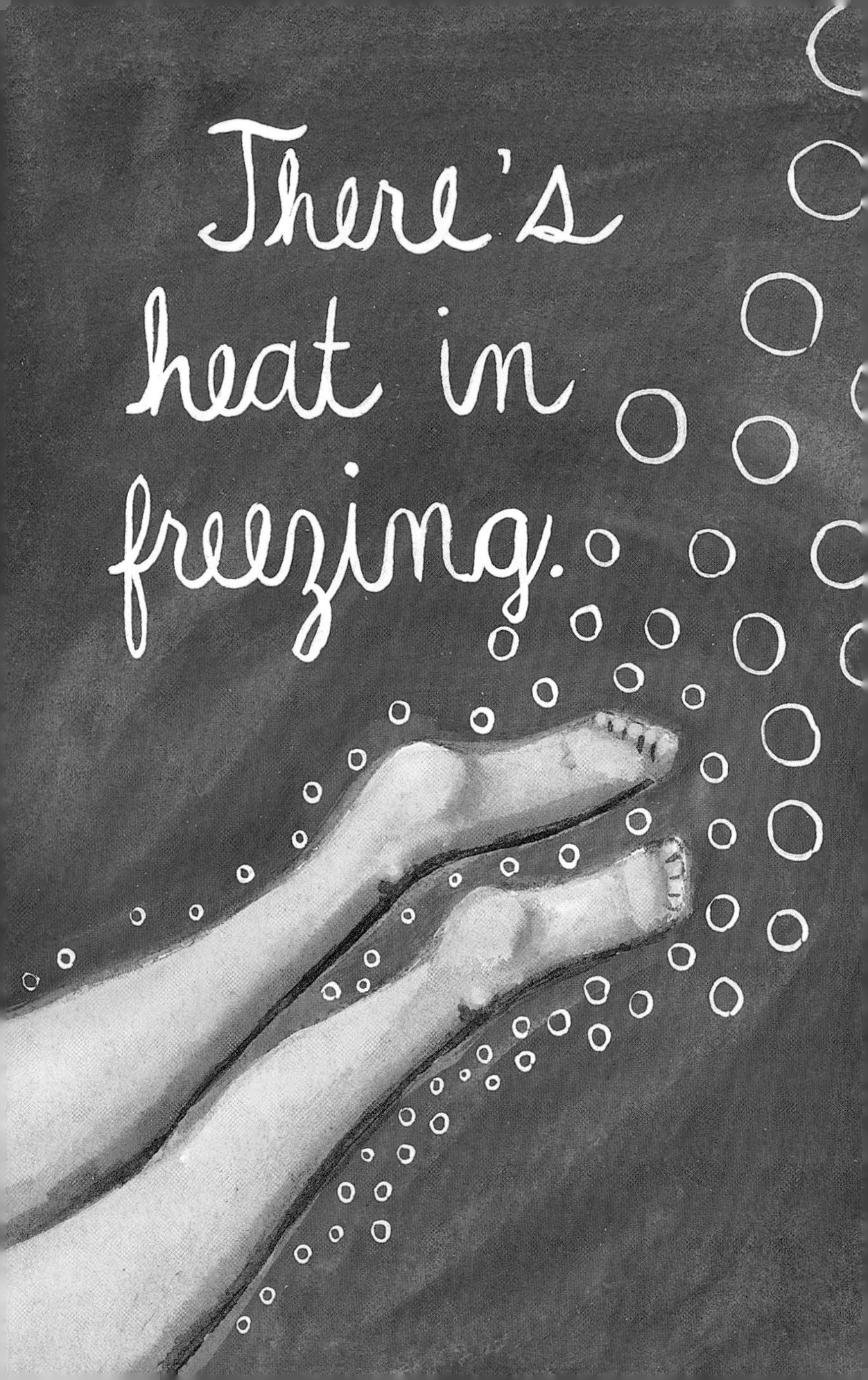
There's heat in freezing.

About the Author

Tanya Davis is a Canadian singer-songwriter-poet. Since bursting onto the Halifax music scene in 2006 with her debut, "Make a List," Tanya has garnered praise from the music industry, her audience, and her peers, as well as multiple award nominations including the 2009 ECMA Female Recording of the Year for her sophomore release, "Gorgeous Morning."

www.tanyadavis.ca

About the Illustrator

Andrea Dorfman works as a filmmaker, animator, cinematographer, and artist. A graduate of McGill University and the Nova Scotia College of Art and Design, she has directed two feature films, "Parsley Days" (2000) and "Love That Boy" (2003), as well as numerous short films including the Emmy Award-nominated animation "Flawed" (2010).

www.andreadorfman.com